this is Shrewsbury

Authors: Al Smith, Mike Ashton and Danny Beath

Editors: Fay Easton and Phil Northwood

Publisher: Shrewsbury Town Centre Management Partnership

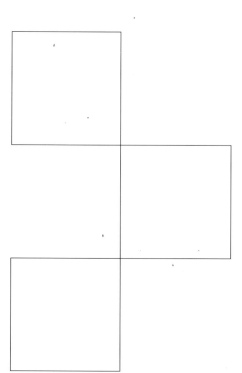

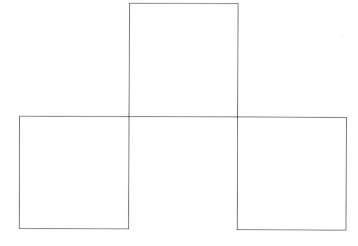

this is Shrewsbury

Published by Shrewsbury Town Centre Management Partnership

Victorian Wing, 20 Dogpole, Shrewsbury, Shropshire SY1 1ES, United Kingdom

Email: info@stcmp.com • www.stcmp.com

First published 2003

A catalogue record for this book is available from the British Library

ISBN 0-9545548-0-9

Principal Photography: Danny Beath, Chris Nottingham, Mike Ashton, Ben Osborne

Printed by Livesey Limited, 101 Longden Road, Shrewsbury, Shropshire SY3 9EB.

- 21st century living in a priceless historic setting
- splendid River Severn vistas
- open parks
- sweeping Georgian terraces
- unique shops
- intimate night clubs
- great restaurants, bars and cafés
- old fashioned pubs

… great town… great people… *This is Shrewsbury – a way of life*

Early morning at Kingsland Bridge by Danny Beath

Rob Thompson in Brady's Bar, Castle Foregate by Chris Nottingham

shrewsbury is...

in bloom

shrewsbury is...

leafy

Shrewsbury has over 260 acres of parks and open spaces

The Quarry Park covers 29 acres

Dr Johnson visiting in 1774
did much admire the avenue of trees
in the Quarry Park

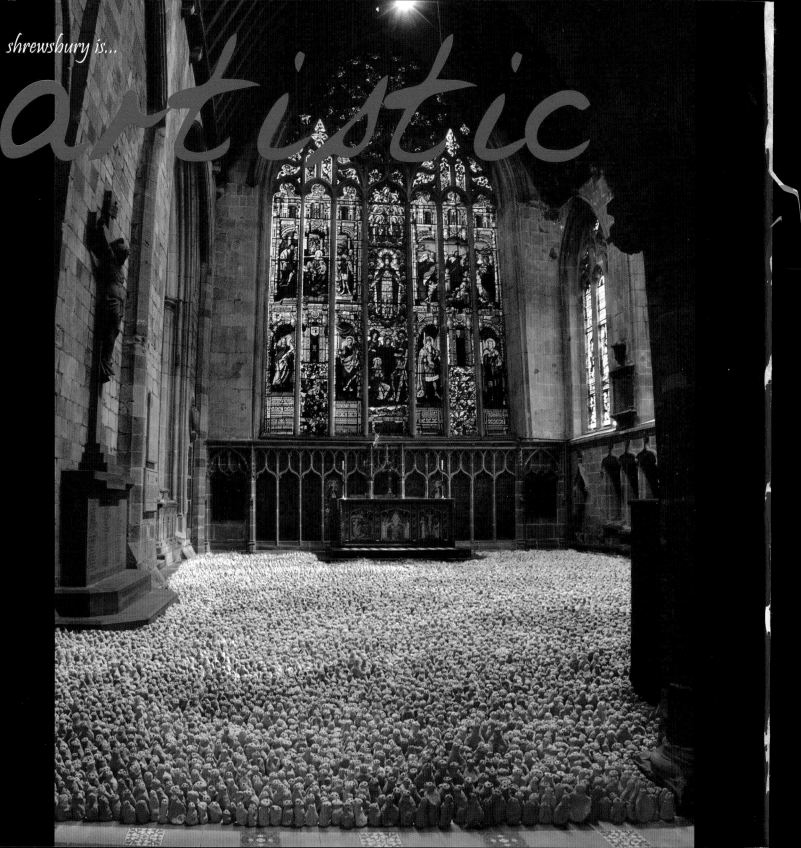

shrewsbury is...

artistic

A thousand years ago an artist carved a dove in the Benedictine Abbey. Five hundred years ago mermaids were carved onto an archway. In the year 2000 a stainless steel face sits on top of a newel post.

It is amongst this visually rich backdrop that contemporary artists have quietly flourished. Galleries have sprung up, exciting exhibition programmes developed and major events have been staged.

Dew Pattern by Chris Parsons

200 foot White Tiger, part of the Visual Arts Festival

Field for the British Isles when at St Mary's Church

Come and discover the visual arts in Shrewsbury. Whether you are strolling around and looking at carvings, statues and sculptures, visiting challenging contemporary exhibitions, thinking about buying fine antique paintings through to modern master prints, you will find it here. Even if you stop for a coffee, a lot of our cafés have displays by local artists.

Thirty Foot Fish in a Deck Chair by Ron Gerhardt, Shirl Barre, Jim Sadler, Maggie Allmark, and Jane Wilson

Mansers Fine Paintings

RealArt Gallery

Shrewsbury Museum & Art Gallery

There are numerous galleries to be found throughout Shrewsbury. You can find 19th century paintings at Manser Callaghan, contemporary craft and artwork at The RealArt Gallery and major contemporary exhibitions at Shrewsbury Museum & Art Gallery.

Giant Flowers by Jacqueline Leech, one of the many works which can regularly be found at the Darwin Shopping Centre

27 1ST
Daily Mail, Friday, August 3, 2001

Abbey artist portrays the crucifixion w

The image of Christ that's deemed too disturbing for children

By **David Wilkes**

IT is meant to lay bare Christ's suffering on the cross.

But a sculpture depicting him naked and decomposing has been condemned as too graphic and disturbing.

Visitors to Shrewsbury Abbey, where the work is on show, have described it as frightening and unsuitable for children.

Others have branded the 7ft image of Christ obscene and disturbing.

The Naked Christ, created by Michele Coxon and named after Michelangelo's famous sculpture, is made from sheep bones, rusty bits of metal, tissue paper and resin.

Christ's ribs are clearly visible through his rotting flesh, and he wears a crown of thorns made from barbed wire.

Although he is in a crucifixion pose, there is no cross. Instead, the sculpture is attached directly to a pillar.

Miss Coxon, also a children's author and illustrator, decided to try her hand at sculpture after completing an art course at college.

She is currently in the U.S. promoting her latest book.

There is an explanation of her work on a plaque by the work, which hangs in the north aisle of the abbey's Norman knave. 'The

A study in suffering: The Naked Christ has n

materials I have used are all found on my walks along the River Vyrnwy and around the fields of Meifod, Wales, where I live,' she writes.

'The wood is worn, softened and shaped by the water. Metal is left abandoned by farmers to turn the colour of autumn rust.

'The bones of dead sheep are picked clean by crows and wild foxes and scavenged by the wind.

'To pass a carcass day after day, watching it slowly decay and

return to my art.

'When Christ I d but over t the right

'By ther need a p

'I want who ha earthly animals flown bu

The s two-we

artistic

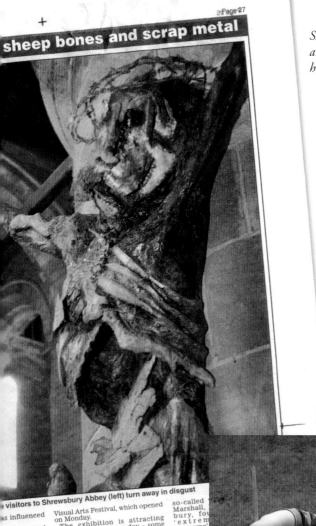

sheep bones and scrap metal

Shrewsbury's art hits the headlines

...visitors to Shrewsbury Abbey (left) turn away in disgust

...as influenced
...The Naked
...o have a cross
...could not find
...od.
...that I did not
...s.
...age of a man
...d and whose
...aying, like the
...s. The soul has

...s part of the
...l Shrewsbury

Visual Arts Festival, which opened on Monday.
The exhibition is attracting around 500 visitors a day – some of whom have left the abbey in disgust.
Sarah Burns, 34, from Shrewsbury, who visited the exhibition yesterday, said: 'I'm glad I didn't bring my children along. The statue is obscene.
'It is very gory. It made me wince when I first laid eyes on it.
'I find it disturbing that a church would choose to display this

so-called
Marshall,
bury, fou...
'extrem...
gruesome'...
Abbey...
Knight s...
mixed rea...
'Many v...
shown the...
of crucifix...
'It is a v...
and unde...
some peo...
d...

One of Shrewsbury's budding artists

Some artists working in Shrewsbury today

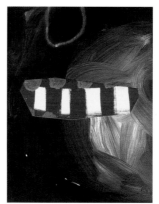

Steve Vicary

Ann McCay

Carl Jaycock

Jane Wilson

Judith Moy

Al Smith

shrewsbury is...

fest

Shrewsbury has a good time,
all year round!

Shrewsbury enjoys:

Festival of Shopping	January
Darwin Festival	February
Children's Book Festival	May
Shrewsbury Rowing Regatta	May
Shrewsbury Carnival	June
Kite & Boomerang Festival	June
West Mid Agricultural Show	June
Shrewsbury Green Festival	July
International Music Festival	July
World Music Day	July
This is Art Festival	July
Shrewsbury Flower Show	August
Steam Rally	August
Real Ale Festival	September
Heritage Open Days	September
Christmas Lights	November
Christmas Carols in the Square	December

shrewsbury is...
building

Old St Chad's Church

Saxon foundation

Shrewsbury Castle

Norman foundation

Timber Framed

Abbot's House, c.1450

Jacobean Brick

Rowley's Mansion, 1618

Caroleon Stone

Library, 1630

Queen Anne

Bowdler House, 1713

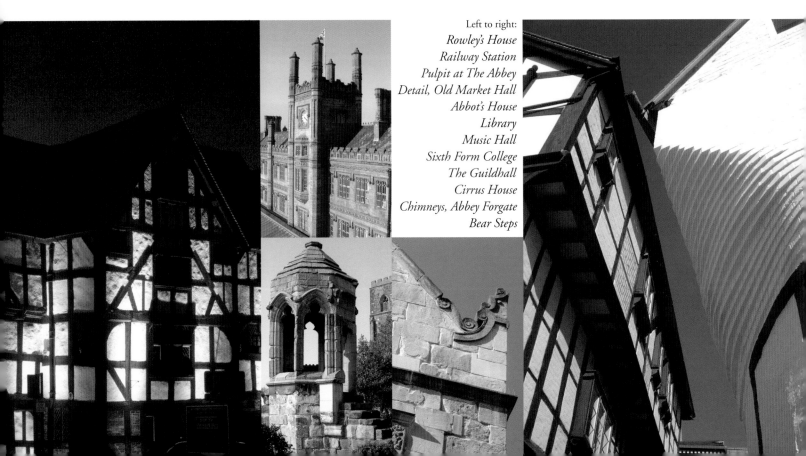

Left to right:
*Rowley's House
Railway Station
Pulpit at The Abbey
Detail, Old Market Hall
Abbot's House
Library
Music Hall
Sixth Form College
The Guildhall
Cirrus House
Chimneys, Abbey Forgate
Bear Steps*

Wander around Shrewsbury and you will see over 600 listed buildings and award winning contemporary structures, telling the story of architecture over one thousand years

Edwardian

Former Hospital, 1908

Art Deco

Shelton Road, 1930s

Pre-fab

Monkmoor, 1950s

Folk

Coal Merchants

Concrete

Lloyds Bank, 1965

Contemporary

Mansers Antiques

shrewsbury is...
Curious

THE XV DAY OF IVNE WAS THIS BVYLDING BEGONN WILLIAM IONES AND THOMAS CHARLTON GENT THEN BAYLIFFES AND WAS ERECTED AND COVERED IN THEIR TIME

On the north gable of the Old Market Hall stands an ancient statue that was brought here from its original site on the now demolished old Welsh Bridge. Although everyone agrees it represents a highly important figure, no-one is quite sure who. Arguments revolve around the possibilities of Edward I and the Duke of York, father of Edward IV.

The Holy Grail is claimed to have been found at nearby Hawkstone Park.

Our giant Town Crier

All over Shrewsbury you can find the Loggerheads coat of arms although no-one is quite sure why.

John Mytton, eccentric MP for Shrewsbury in 1820, set fire to his shirt to cure hiccups.

August 12, 1996

HOLY EGG-CUP!
'Grail' found in attic
REBECCA MAER

THIS is the Holy Grail ... straight from an attic in the Midlands!

That is the remarkable claim of amateur historian Dr Graham Phillips. And even though the onyx goblet looks more like an egg-cup it is just two inches high, he swears it is the vessel used by Christ at the Last Supper.

Novelty

The Coventry-based psychologist explains: "If someone were going to make a fake, it would be more likely to be an elaborate chalice and not something like this little cup."

Then, after it was dated by the British Museum as possibly Roman, the 24-year-old graphic designer lodged the prize in a bank vault.

For Dr Phillips, 41, convinced her it is the Marian Chalice found by the Christian empress Helena inside Christ's sepulchre and used by

from it would become immortal. But the "relic" is now owned by Victoria Palmer, of Rugby, Warwicks, who thought she just had a Victorian novelty in her loft.

Mary Magdalene and Joseph of Arimathea to collect Jesus's blood.

In his book The Search for the Grail published next week, Dr Phillips says the goblet was brought to Britain when Rome was sacked by the barbarians in 410 AD.

In 1190, a Welsh monk rescued to it as being in the possession of the heirs of the last king of Powys.

Dr Phillips says a later descendant of the same family, Squire Walter Langham, found the cup hidden in Hawkstone Park near Shrewsbury in 1920. Ms Palmer is his great grand-daughter.

Dixons

TOP BRAND
MOBILES

TOT GNAWE
BY A RA

Throughout the myriad of timber framed buildings in the town centre you can spot interesting carvings, but none more so than those above Costa Coffee café on the corner of High Street and Grope Lane. During its 1990 restoration, old rotten beams were replaced with new oak showing contemporary issues, including traffic problems and the Poll Tax with imagery of Thatcher and Heseltine.

The nearby ruined Roman city of Viroconium at Wroxeter was one of the largest sites in the country, with living standards far higher than almost anywhere in Europe. If ever a sustained archaeological dig takes place, who knows what treasures may be unearthed? Only by visiting the site museum and Shrewsbury Museum and Art Gallery can you get a glimpse of what may be.

In 1953, Sir Edmund Hilary and Sherpa Tenzing were the first to officially climb Mount Everest. However, in 1933 George Mallory and his partner Andrew 'Sandy' Irving were lost near the summit. Sandy Irving was a pupil at Shrewsbury School from 1916 to 1921 and remained in close contact with Shrewsbury for all his short life. Recently, Mallory's body was found, but Irving's is still missing. It is believed, or hoped, that when Irving is found his camera will show proof that he and Mallory were the first to ascend the highest mountain in the world – *or were they?*

Rowland Lee's extraordinary career saw him become the Bishop of Coventry and Lichfield and Lord President of the Council in the Marches. He oversaw the hanging of 5,000 men in the space of six years; he was the friend and servant of Thomas Cromwell and Henry VIII. He officiated at the marriage between Henry VIII and Anne Boleyn and worked for Cardinal Wolsey. In 1533 he was referred to as an *"Earthly beast, a mole and an enemy to all godly learning"*. He died in Shrewsbury in 1543 and was buried before the altar of Old St Chad's church.

Roman finger, at Shrewsbury Museum & Art Gallery

Let this small Monument record the name
Of CADMAN, and to future times proclaim
How by'n attempt to fly from this high spire
Across the Sabrine stream he did acquire
His fatal end. 'Twas not for want of skill
Or courage to perform the task he fell:
No, no, a faulty Cord being drawn too tight
Hurried his Soul on high to take her flight
Which bid the Body here beneath good Night.
Feb'y 2nd 1739 aged 28.

On St Mary's Church

> # The crookedest black and white houses, all of many shapes except straight shapes

Charles Dickens, while staying in Shrewsbury

This is Shrewsbury – a beautiful English town in the country and a real shoppers paradise

shopping

All the shops, cafés, bars and galleries you could wish for, set in a compact commercial centre encircled by glorious river and parkland. Shrewsbury is the largest retail centre in the region and the only one where you can still see kingfishers, otters and sparrowhawks.

In Shrewsbury you can buy everything you've ever needed – and many things you didn't know you needed.

One million square feet of shopping and more shops than Bluewater, Europe's biggest shopping mall. Many of Shrewsbury's shops are unique. Independent shops located in classic shopping streets, leafy town squares, secret shuts and passages and in 21st century malls.

KUKADÄSS

- Bespoke furniture
- Designer frocks
- Hand made hats
- Decorated wellies
- Live snakes
- Hand rolled Cuban cigars
- Nuts, bolts and kitchen sinks

urban

Urban is a state of mind, a way of behaving – to some it conjures up street warriors, to others it's doing lunch... Shrewsbury takes it easy over a coffee.

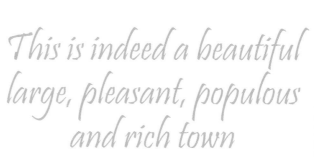

This is indeed a beautiful large, pleasant, populous and rich town

Daniel Defoe

GUCCI
made in Italy

choice

Mulberry
ENGLAND

*City centre,
designer-chic in an
historic county town*

LOUIS VUITTON
MALLETIER A PARIS

MAISON FONDÉE EN 1854

Château
Mouton Rothschild
1982

ROLEX

TONI&GUY

CHIEMSEE

ALESSI

DKNY

JAEGER

Monsoon

☞ **Tahitian Black Pearls**
@ JA Woodroffe, Mardol

☞ Hand Rolled **Cuban Cigars**
@ Adlards, Shoplatch

☞ **Embroidered Silks**
@ Interiors with Bryony
Cooper, St Mary's Street

☞ **Alessi** @ Live Easy,
7/8 Dogpole

☞ **Prada** @ Pockets in
The Square

☞ **Aquascutum**
@ Majors, Claremont Street

☞ **D&G** @ Shoe-b-do,
The Parade Shopping Centre

☞ **Miss Sixty** @ Rackhams,
High Street

☞ **Mulberry** @ Finishing Touch,
High Street

☞ **Gucci** & **DKNY**
@ Ernest Jones,
Darwin Shopping Centre

☞ **Rolex** & **Fabergé**
@ Goldsmiths in the Square

☞ **Naim** @ Creative Audio,
Dogpole

☞ **Beluga Caviar**
@ Christopher's Fine Foods,
Mardol

☞ **Adini** @ Adini.
St Alkmund's Square

☞ **Burberry** @ The Dresser,
Roushill

☞ **Jaguar** @ Hartwell,
Old Potts Way

☞ **Mercedes** @ Mercedes-Benz,
Battlefield Road

☞ **Alpine** @ SMC,
St Michael's Street

☞ **Fine wines** @ Tanners,
Wyle Cop

shrewsbury is...

Ajar

Chester Street

Town Walls

Dogpole

St Mary's Church

Quarry Place

Sutton Road

St John's Hill

Butcher Row

Dogpole

The Castle

College Hill

School Gardens

Town Walls

Longden Coleham   *Castle Foregate*   *Belmont*   *College Hill*   *College Hill*

St Alkmund's Square   *Belmont*   *School Gardens*   *College Hill*

School Gardens   *Town Walls*   *Castle Foregate*   *School Gardens*   *Castle Gates*   *The Castle*

bookish

Shrewsbury and Shropshire have given a wealth of literary inspiration to writers though the ages. Maybe stay awhile and write the next great novel yourself.

- Wilfred Owen, born in nearby Oswestry, lived in Shrewsbury.
- Arthur Conan Doyle lived in nearby Ruyton-XI-Towns.
- Charles Dickens visited and performed in Shrewsbury
- Samuel Taylor Coleridge read at the Unitarian Church in 1798.
- Private Eye started life as a student magazine at Shrewsbury School by pupils Richard Ingrams and Willie Rushton.

Shropshire's County Library is housed within the magnificent former Shrewsbury School, dating from the 1590's.

If you want to buy books, you can visit any of the independent, chain, budget or charity shops, as well as book fairs and antiquarian outlets – in Shrewsbury you can find virtually any title you've ever wanted...

shrewsbury is...
learned

If your choice is state or private education, then school children can only but flourish in Shrewsbury

However, it is the safe and rich environment of Shrewsbury that allows children to learn much more than just the three R's.

Of course, age is no barrier to education. In Shrewsbury the life long learning ethos is encouraged at every turn. You can study many topics from a one-off afternoon course, to a full blown degree. See what's on offer at the Gateway Education & Arts Centre, the Shrewsbury Learning Centre, the Sixth Form College and Shrewsbury College of Arts & Technology (SCAT). Or you could just pick up a copy of 'Ace' magazine which lists all the courses available.

Above the entrance archway to the library stand two stone statues dating from 1627. The figures represent a scholar and graduate called Philomathon and Polymathon. Between them reads a quotation from Socrates "If you are a lover of learning, you will become very learned".

A graduate from the University of Birmingham at The Gateway, Chester Street

Shrewsbury Old Boys

Charles Darwin (Botanist and Heretic)

Wilfred Owen (Poet)

Michael Palin (All round Good Egg)

William Wycherley (Dramatist)

George Jeffreys (Judge)

Michael Hestletine (Politician)

Willie Rushton (Writer)

Richard Ingrams (Journalist)

John Peel (Broadcaster)

Paul Foot (Journalist)

were all educated in Shrewsbury

Half Learned

When a timber-framed building is first constructed, the carpenter marks the joints with Roman numerals to ensure the right piece fits in the right place. Shrewsbury buildings show that Tudor craftsmen didn't quite get the hang of the concept. Abbot's House in Butcher Row as one example, has iiiv (8) and iiiiv (9).

shrewsbury is...

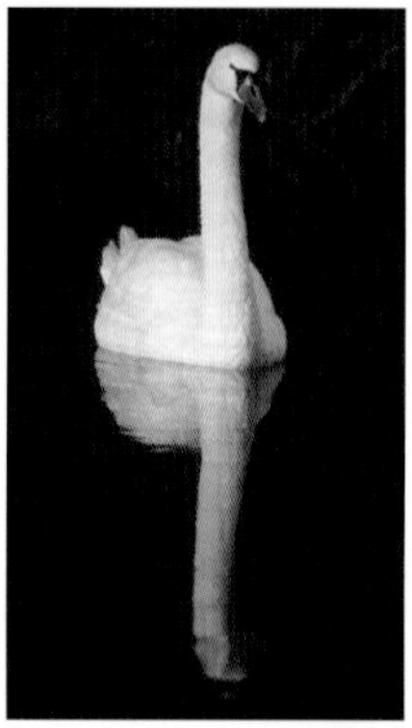

Swimming along –
Swimming along –
Swimming along from Severn
And paying a call at Dawley Bank
while Swimming along to heaven

John Betjeman (1940)

awash

During the first part
of the 19th century
any boys from
Shrewsbury School
found boating on the
river were flogged

Kingsland Bridge

There is a gentle nymph not far from hence,
The moist curb sways the smooth Severn stream;
Sabrina is her name, a virgin pure...

John Milton (1608 – 1674)

*Sabrina, goddess of the
River Severn, to be found
in the Dingle*

Conduit Head at Radbrook fed water through
wooden pipes of elm, to reservoirs around the town.

Victorian cast iron drinking fountains can be found
around the town, one of which is on Town Walls.

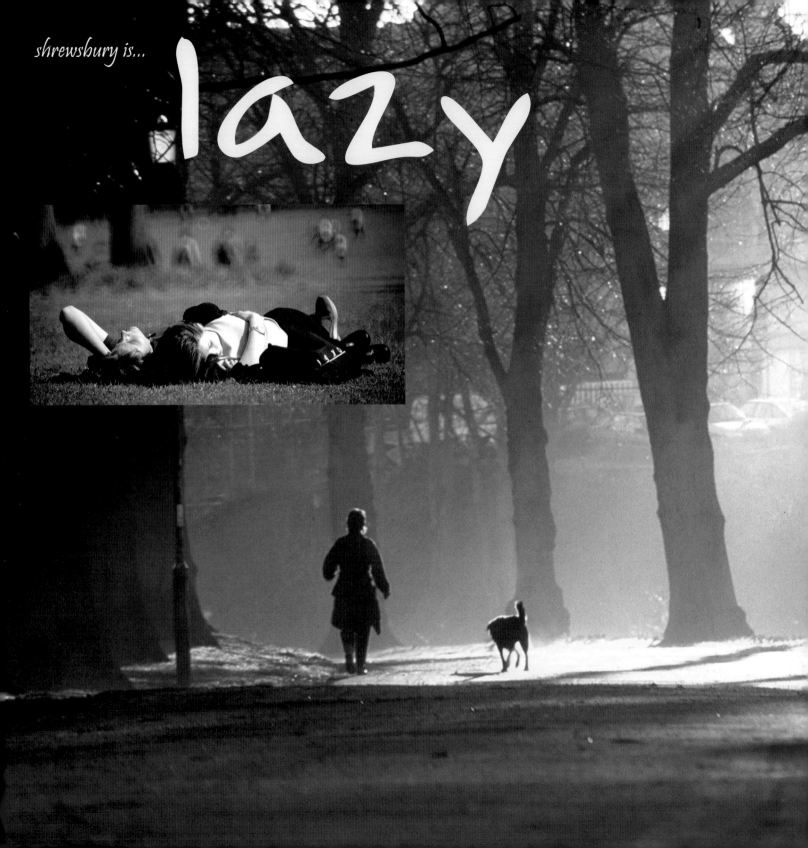

shrewsbury is...

lazy

TOTAL 135

WKTS 4

OVERS 37

LAST INNS 130

shrewsbury is...

de lic

In Shrewsbury you can indulge your taste buds with food from around the world

British

French

Japanese

Italian

Mexican

Chinese

Thai

Indian

Mongolian...

You could try over 30 quality restaurants, if you add cafés, takeaways, sandwich bars, coffee shops and pubs you'll probably have to diet for the rest of your life.

the middle of one side ; fold the other over it, and pinch it up into a somewhat oval shape ; flatten it with your hand at the top, letting the seam be quite at the bottom ; rub the tops over with the white of an egg, laid on with a brush, and dust loaf sugar over the top ; bake in a moderate oven.

MINCEMEAT FOR BANBURY CAKES.—Beat up a quarter of a pound of butter until it becomes in the state of cream ; then mix with it half a pound of candied orange and lemon peel, cut fine ; one pound of currants, a quarter of an ounce of ground cinnamon ; and a quarter of an ounce of allspice ; mix all well together, and keep in a jar till wanted for use.

SHREWSBURY CAKES.—Take half a pound of flour ; a quarter of a pound of sugar ; the same of butter and enough egg well beaten to mix it ; grate in some nutmeg, mix well, roll thin, cut with a pastry cutter or wineglass, and bake on buttered paper, or in a greased and floured tin.

CHEESE CAKES.—Beat a quarter of a pound of butter with the hand in a warm pan until it becomes creamy.

BATH BUNS.—A quarter of a pound of flour ; four yolks and three whites of eggs, with four teaspoonfuls of solid fresh yeast. Beat in a bowl, and set before the fire to rise ; then rub into one pound of flour ten ounces of butter ; put in half a pound of sugar, and caraway comfits ; when the eggs and yeast are pretty light, mix by degrees altogether ; throw a cloth over it, and set before the fire to rise. Make the buns, and when on the tins, brush over with the yolk of egg and milk ; strew them with caraway comfits ; bake in a quick oven. If baking powder is used instead of yeast, use two teaspoonfuls, and proceed as directed, omitting to set the dough before the fire to rise, which is useless as regards all articles made with baking powder.

BATH BUNS (another recipe).—
Ingredients.—One pound of flour, three ounces of butter, three ounces of sugar, one ounce of D.C.L. yeast, half a pint of milk, one egg.
Method.—Rub flour, sugar, and butter together. Beat up the egg,

A BLUE CHEESE

MUSTARD & BEER

ED WITH CHEST

GETABLE W

RAVY

& ROSEMARY

CHEESE

IED TOMATO

PIG TROUGH

AMERICAN

shrewsbury is...

quaffing

There are sixty pubs and bars in Shrewsbury Town Centre

From a relaxing riverside drink to a lively night out, Shrewsbury has a pub or bar to meet every taste and occasion.

The floors inside the Wyle Cop premises of **Tanners Wine Merchants** were all made specially for the rolling of casks which used to be brought from the railway station by horse and cart. These casks started their journey in Jamaica, Guyana, Ireland, Bordeaux, Jerez and Oporto and were mostly shipped to Liverpool and on by rail to Shrewsbury.

When Charles Dickens stayed at the Lion Hotel and wrote about the crooked roofs he could see, he was probably looking at Tanners.

Many of the town's pubs are consistantly found in the Good Beer and Good Pub Guides.

The King's Head, in Mardol (built in 1457), boasts an ancient painting of the last supper.

Shrewsbury Real Ale Festival is held annually in September.

Shrewsbury boasts two fine breweries, The Salopian Brewery and The Dolphin Inn & Brewery.

There are many other award winning breweries nearby including: Hanby Ales, Wem; Hobson's Brewery, Cleobury Mortimer; Wood's Brewery, Wistanstow; Corvedale Brewery, Craven Arms; Six Bells, Bishop's Castle.

The Golden Cross, off High Street, dates back to 1428 and was formerly the Sacristan's quarters for old St Chad's. In the 18th century, during very long sermons (sometimes lasting two hours) church wardens would seek refuge in this pub.

As well as a selection of fine ales, spirits and wines, the Three Fishes in Fish Street is a no-smoking pub.

The Old Lion Tap was once a tap room to the Lion Hotel where the servants quaffed.

Wroxter Roman Vineyard is one of the world's most northerly red wine producers. The five varieties of grape grown here produce award winning wines.

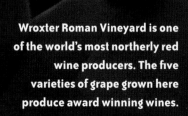

performance

There is a rich history of performance in Shrewsbury, from 1180 AD when the 'Shrewsbury Fragments', parts of Christmas and Easter plays, were performed in church, to 1495 AD when Prince Arthur attended the Whitsuntide theatrical production in the 'Dry Dingle' (now the municipal swimming pool). The whole tradition of English panto can be traced back to Shrewsbury born John Weaver (1673-1760). Charles Dickens performed in a play at the Music Hall in 1852 and returned to give a reading in 1858. Laurel & Hardy appeared at what is now a bingo hall for a week-long run.

Many other stars appeared at the now Bingo Hall including The Beatles. Apparently, Pink Floyd played at Shrewsbury College of Arts and Technology and Led Zeppelin played an acoustic set at the Bear Steps during the height of their fame.

Today the Music Hall is the main theatre, showing a very diverse range of performances covering music, comedy, dance and plays. It is hoped that a new theatre will be built in the near future.

hot&
sweaty

this is shrewsbury...

Porthill Bridge

shrewsbury is...

fire & brimstone

Like most towns, if you sniff their soft underbelly you will start to find the nasty bits

Mardol – "The Devil's Limit"

MARDOL

During 1894 a band of citizens were organising the commission of a memorial statue to Darwin. In the same year the spire of St Mary's Church collapsed, leaving the Vicar in no doubt of God's will demonstrating against the blasphemous Theory of Evolution.

In 1814, William Wheeler was hanged on Shrewsbury gallows for committing an "unnatural" offence.

Ghost tours of the town are run regularly – particularly around Halloween. Contact Tourist Information for details.

During the 19th century an official report of the horrid goings on at Shrewsbury's Flaxmill was presented to Parliament and this dark satanic mill was brought to account.

SHROPSHIRE MALTINGS

Atop the nearby Stiperstones sits *'The Devil's Chair'*; it is said that anybody sitting here will be cursed.

Claims of ghostly goings on can be found throughout Shrewsbury and Shropshire. Perhaps the most famous case is the photograph of a ghost standing in a blazing

doorway of Wem Town Hall as it burnt to the ground. The international media spread the story around the world; it was reported in April 1996 that the photograph was not a hoax.

bloody

During the late 13th century, Edward I became known as "the Hammer of the Scots" and has recently become infamous for his depiction subjugating William 'Braveheart' Wallace. However, before turning to Scotland he first had to crush Wales. In 1282, Welsh Llewelyn II led an uprising against the English but was swiftly defeated and beheaded. Shortly after, his brother David was captured and brought to Shrewsbury Abbey to stand before King Edward and his Parliament. David was put to death – he was hung, drawn and quartered at the High Cross on Castle Gates. His head was taken to the Tower of London and impaled on a spike next to his brother's.

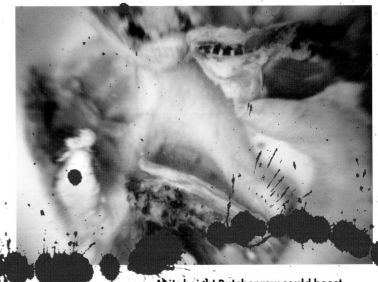

At its height Butcher row could boast 16 butchers shops. With no abattoir available untill 1911, livestock was butchered in the street. Blood would run along the gutters.

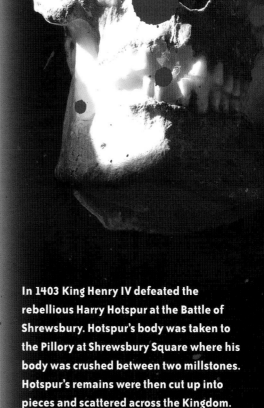

This skull, found at the site of St Austin's Friary, has a sword cut above its eye socket and dates from the Battle of Shrewsbury. It is housed at Shrewsbury Museum & Art Gallery.

All old towns have a bloody past, but few as bloody as Shrewsbury's

SCENE : *England.*

castle.

gues.

of you

umour

vest,
unfold
arth. 5
s ride,
pounce,
eports.
y, sil
y
efence,
e other

tyrant

pipe 15

Blown by surmise. jealousies, conjectures,
And of so easy and so plain a stop
That the blunt monster with uncounted
heads,
The still-discordant wav'ring multitude,
Can play upon it. But what need I thus 20
My well-known body to anatomize
Among my household? Why is Rumour
here?
I run before King Harry's victory,
Who, in a bloody field by Shrewsbury,
Hath beaten down young Hotspur and his
troops, 25
Quenching the flame of bold rebellion
Even with the rebels' blood. But what
mean I
To speak so true at first? My office is 28
To noise abroad that Harry Monmouth fell
the wrath of noble Hotspur's sword,
And that the Douglas' rage
Stoop'd his anoin d as s deat
This have I rumour'd throug pea
towns
Between that royal field of Shrewsbury 34
And this worm-eaten hold of ragged stone,

In 1403 King Henry IV defeated the rebellious Harry Hotspur at the Battle of Shrewsbury. Hotspur's body was taken to the Pillory at Shrewsbury Square where his body was crushed between two millstones. Hotspur's remains were then cut up into pieces and scattered across the Kingdom.

shrewsbury is...
sanctuary

In January 1938 the Ethiopian Emperor Haile Selassie visited Shrewsbury. His name translates to 'Might of the Trinity'; Rastafarians believe that he will arrange for the deliverance of the black races by procuring for them a homeland in Ethiopia.

The Greek Orthodox 'Church of the Holy Fathers' at Sutton is an early 13th century church built on the foundations of a Saxon church. During July 2000, a major Orthodox Christian millennium festival was staged throughout Shrewsbury with exhibitions, demonstrations, music and food.

Shrewsbury has more than 30 churches

**THE REV. JOHN WESLEY, A.M.
FOUNDER of METHODISM,
PREACHED IN THIS HOUSE
ON HIS FIRST VISIT TO
SHREWSBURY.
MARCH 16TH 1761.**

John Wesley regularly preached in Shrewsbury during the late 18th century.

A medieval stone angel sits on the south gable of the Old Market Hall, brought here from the now demolished Castle Gate. It could date from early 13th century.

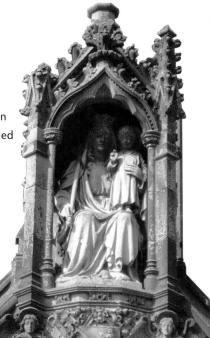

In 1409, King Henry IV and his son Prince Hal (to be Henry V) attended a service at Shrewsbury Abbey.

King Charles I took an oath of Sacrament at St Mary's Church in 1638.

King James II attended a Divine Service at St Mary's Church in 1687.

shrewsbury is...

ahead

shrewsbury is...

Shropshire born Robert Clive laid the foundations for the start of the British Empire in India. Clive of India then returned to live in Shrewsbury and became MP for Shropshire.

The brilliant engineer Thomas Telford was the County Surveyor whose works can be seen throughout Shrewsbury, including his remodelling of The Castle and roadworks adjacent to the Abbey.

Benjamin Disraeli, Prime Minister and friend of Queen Victoria was one of Shrewsbury's two MP's between 1841-1847.

The Flaxmill at Ditherington is the world's first iron framed building. Designed by local Wine Merchant and Surveyor, Charles Bage, this 1796 building saw the birth of design principles that led to the Skyscrapers of New York. Charles is buried at St Chads.

The birth of the House of Commons can be traced to Shrewsbury Abbey where, in 1283, Edward I first invited commoners to sit at his parliament.

The Industrial Revolution was begun in 1709 by Abraham Darby at the nearby World Heritage Site of Ironbridge.

The Theory of Evolution still shakes the world and was conceived by Shrewsbury's most famous son, Charles Dawin.

The modern Olympic Games were founded in 1861 at nearby Much Wenlock by Dr William Penny Brookes. After tireless campaigning, the full Olympic Games as we now know them were adopted in 1896.

John Nash built the earliest Italianate villa in Britain at nearby Cronkhill in 1802.

Clive of India

Cronkhill

The Abbey

inspiRed

The Iron Bridge

Charles Darwin

Laura's Tower by Thomas Telford

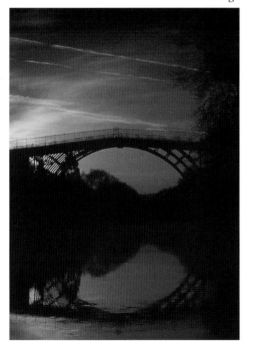

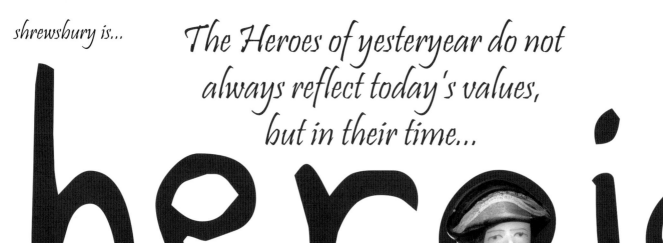

shrewsbury is...

The Heroes of yesteryear do not always reflect today's values, but in their time...

heroic

Admiral John Benbow (1653 – 1702)

A Shrewsbury lad who ran away to sea and become the Nelson of his times. In his early years he fought Moorish Pirates in the Mediterranean, from where his illustrious career took him to the Caribbean to fight the French in 1701. There aboard his lone ship he faced the enemy and was seriously wounded with chain-shot injuries to his legs. He goes down as a genuine British hero whose name was even recorded on a Tavern sign in Robert Louis Stevenson's *'Treasure Island'*. Naval seamen sang to his glories:

"Come all you brave fellows, wherever you be, and drink to the health of our King and Queen, and another good health to the girls that we know, and a third for remembrance of brave Admiral Benbow".

Sir Philip Sydney (1554 – 1586)

A Shrewsbury School Old Boy who was a soldier, poet and scholar. His famous words *"Thy need is greater than mine"* were uttered to a dying soldier, to whom he offered his cup of water. Sir Philip died of his wounds in Holland at the town of Zutphen, now the twin-town of Shrewsbury.

Lord Hill's Column –
The world's largest
Doric Column,
standing at
133¹/₂ feet high

Lord Rowland Hill
(1772 –1842)

Born at Prees Hall, Rowland became one of Britain's most celebrated military men. Second-in-command to the Duke of Wellington, Lieutenant General Hill led the charge of his Light Brigade at Waterloo. Queen Victoria's mother called him *"Our old and esteemed friend"*. In Shrewsbury his statue can be seen atop Lord Hills Column; it was said that he was *"Salopia's Pride and England's Glory"*.

My friend, you would not
tell with such high zest
To children ardent for some
desperate glory
The old lie:

DULCE ET DECORUM EST

PRO PATRIA MORI

Shrewsbury's Wilfred Owen – First World War Poet

shrewsbury is...

grave

EBENEZER SCROOGE

Two gravestones from
Wroxeter Roman
City, now housed in
Rowley's House
Museum

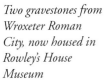

St Chad's Churchyard

A memorial to
Wilfred Owen,
WW1 poet

A Templar Grave at St Eata's Church, Atcham

Graveyard at Battlefield Church

Charles Bage, Architect of the Flaxmill, the precursor to the modern day skyscraper, is buried at St Chad's Church

ered to the Memory of
ARLES BAGE Esq.
arted this Li[f]e Dec.r 30.th 182
aged 70.
GE wido[w] [o]f the above

Art Deco at Battlefield Church

Francis Walford, client for John Nash's Cronkhill, at St Eata's Church, Atcham

Further afield, at nearby Meifod, a skull and crossbones gravestone, and Trefonen (below left) near Oswestry

IN MEMORY OF
FIVE CHILDREN OF
ONATHAN & MARY SIDES
HO WERE BURIED HERE
OMAS on the 26th of May 1831
Aged 1½ Year.
DWARD on the 1st of Oct.r 1833
Aged 3 Months.
LIZ.th on the 28th of Oct.r 1836.
Aged 5 Weeks.
ARRIETT on the 28th Jan.y 1840
Aged 10 Months.
NNE on the 23d of Nov.r 184.

regal

Shrewsbury's very rich history has seen many royal associations over the centuries

The following complete list of recognised Kings and Queens of Britain highlights those that recognised Shrewsbury during their lives.

Egbert	802-839	
Ethelwulf	839-855	
Ethelbald	855-860	
Ethelbert	860-866	
Ethelred	866-871	

Alfred The Great   871-899   The daughter of Alfred ruled West Mercia with her husband Ethelred II. Evidence shows that they constructed a fort at Shrewsbury.

Edward the Elder   899-925

Athelstan   925 – 939   In 925AD Athelstan established a Royal Mint at Shrewsbury.

Edmund   939 – 946   Produced coins from the Shrewsbury Mint.

Eadred   946-955   Produced coins from the Shrewsbury Mint.

Eadwig   955-959   Produced coins from the Shrewsbury Mint.

Edgar   959-975   Refounded St Mary's Church in 960 AD and St Alkmund's as a college.

Edward the Martyr   975-978

Ethelred Unraed   978 – 1016   Pursued by Vikings, he travelled to Shrewsbury in 1006. In 1007 he resigned the government of Mercia to his son-in-law, Aedric, who lived in Shrewsbury from time to time.

Edmund Ironside   1016   Edmund's army devastated the County of Shropshire and visited Shrewsbury.

Cnut   1016-1035   This Viking King produced coins from The Shrewsbury Mint. He married the late King Ethelred's widow, Emma, in 1017.

Harold I   1035 – 1040   Produced coins in Shrewsbury.

Harthacnut   1040-1042   Produced coins in Shrewsbury.

Edward the Confessor   1042 – 1066   Produced coins in Shrewsbury.

Harold II	**1066**	Produced coins in Shrewsbury.
William I	**1066-1087**	Would probably have visited his trusted friend, Roger de Montgomery, the Earl of Shrewsbury.
William Rufus II	**1087-1100**	Produced coins from the Shrewsbury Mint.
Henry I	**1100-1135**	On becoming King, one of his first acts was to marry a descendant of Alfred the Great. His daughter and sole heir Matilda, visited Shrewsbury with the King in 1102. The Castle became a royal fortress in which Henry and Matilda regularly stayed. In 1126 he gave the town its first Charter and presented the town to his second wife, Adeliza.

Stephen   **1135-1154**

After Henry's death, his heir Matilda declared herself Queen, however his nephew Stephen was crowned King. In 1138, King Stephen marched to Shrewsbury to besiege the Castle held by Matilda's men. After four weeks, the town was taken. The civil unrest is finally resolved when Stephen accepted Matilda's son, Henry Plantagenet, as his own adopted son and heir.

Henry II   **1154-1189**

Henry Plantagenet is described as one of the most remarkable figures in History. In 1158, he passed through Shrewsbury on an expedition to Wales. Whilst in Shrewsbury he ordered the Castle to be re-built in stone. He also reduced the local taxes by half.

Richard 1 the Lionheart   **1189-1199**

In 1189 Richard gave Shrewsbury its oldest surviving Charter.

John	**1199-1216**	In 1199, John gave a further Charter and visited in 1207 and 1216.
Henry III	**1216-1272**	Henry first visited Shrewsbury with his father King John. As King, Henry visited four times between 1220 and 1241, he ordered the construction of the Town Walls. A fifth visit took place in 1267.
Edward I	**1272-1307**	Edward is perhaps best known via Hollywood as the King who subjugated the Scots and defeated William 'Braveheart' Wallace in 1298. Before his attention turned to Scotland, he successfully focused on Wales with the same ferocity and guile, using Shrewsbury as a gateway and base. In 1284, Wales was finally defeated and Edward's son was proclaimed the first English 'Prince of Wales'.

Edward II   **1307-1327**

After his defeat at Bannockburn in 1314, civil war broke out. In 1322 Edward arrived in Shrewsbury issuing an amnesty to all his opponents. Those who accepted this offer came to greet the King and were immediately arrested.

Edward III 1327-1377

Although Edward III did not visit Shrewsbury, his statue can be seen on the exterior of the west Face of Shrewsbury Abbey.

Richard II   **1377-1399**

In 1398, Richard summoned the Great Parliament at Shrewsbury Abbey.

shrewsbury is... regal

Henry IV   **1399-1413**   In 1403 Henry fought the Battle of Shrewsbury.

Henry V **1413-1422**   As Prince Hal he fought alongside his father at the Battle of Shrewsbury.

Henry VI   **1422-1461**

Edward IV **1461-1483**   Whilst living at the Dominican Friary, Edward received news of his father, The Duke of York's, death. Edward set out from Shrewsbury to win the Battle of Mortimer's Cross and was crowned King.

Edward V   **1483**   As Prince Edward, he spent much of his time at the Dominican Friary along with his two younger brothers who were born there. In 1483, after his father died, Edward was proclaimed King and taken to the Tower of London with his brother Richard, to await his Coronation. The Princes in The Bloody Tower were never seen again. It is assumed their uncle, Richard III, had them murdered.

Richard III   **1483-1485**

Henry VII   **1485-1509**   In 1485 Welsh Henry Tudor stayed overnight in Wyle Cop before his triumph at Bosworth Field. He visited again in 1488, 1490 and 1495.

Henry VIII   **1509-1547**   While still a young Prince, his elder brother Arthur married Katherine of Aragon and lived at Shropshire's Ludlow Castle. Arthur visited Shrewsbury from time to time but sadly died a young man. Prince Henry married his brothers widow. A servant of Katherine's, Anthony Rocke lived at the Old House in Dogpole. Although no evidence shows Henry VIII visited Shrewsbury, he did draw up plans for The Abbey to become a Cathedral, which never came to be.

Edward VI   **1547-1553**

Mary I   **1553-1558**   Known as Bloody Mary, she stayed at the Old House in Dogpole as a Princess.

Elizabeth I   **1558-1603**   The Queen began the journey to Shrewsbury to see a theatrical performance at Shrewsbury School, but turned back on hearing of an outbreak of Plague in the town.

James I   **1603-1625**

Charles I   **1625-1649**   In 1642, Charles arrived in Shrewsbury with 8,000 of his men. He stayed for 3 weeks at the Old Council House.

Cromwell   **1649-1660**

Charles II **1660-1685**   After his father's execution, Charles II and his Scottish army entered England. He sent an envoy to Shrewsbury to surrender.

James II   **1685-1689**   In 1687, James visited the Council House in Shrewsbury.

William III   **1689-1702**   Although he did not himself visit, the Dutch William of Orange sent troops to Ireland and they stayed overnight in Shrewsbury. At the Old Dun Cow Inn in Abbey Foregate, they murdered a local 'unprovoked'.

Mary II   **1689-1694**

Anne   **1702-1714**

George I	1714-1727	
George II	1727-1760	
George III	1760-1820	
George IV	**1820-1830**	Although no evidence shows he visited Shrewsbury, his wife Mrs Fitzherbert is associated with a now demolished mansion on Castle Street. Although married, she was a woman of inferior station and by virtue did not acquire a rank or inheritance.
William IV	1830-1837	
Victoria	**1837-1901**	In 1832, Princess Victoria was staying at nearby Pitchford Hall with her mother the Duchess of Kent. They visited Shrewsbury School and Victoria was described as 'A short uninteresting girl in a large leghorn hat'.
Edward VII	1901-1910	
George V	**1910-1936**	In 1914, George visited The Salop Infirmary (now the Parade Shopping Centre) and bestowed the title 'Royal'. In 1927 he visited again with his wife, Queen Mary.
Edward VIII	**1936**	As Prince of Wales, Edward casually flew into the area in 1932 to visit Shrewsbury School.
George VI	1936-1952	
Elizabeth II	**1952**	Her many associations include an October 1952 visit to the Queen's Terrace at Kingsland, the official opening of Shirehall in 1967 and a visit to the West Mid Show in 1975.

Shrewsbury has not only seen British royals grace the town…

Caratacus 43 – 46AD
The son of Cunobelin was the last British King to defy the Romans and was finally defeated at his stronghold on nearby Llanymynech Hill.

Emperor Hadrian 117-138AD
In 122AD Hadrian visited nearby Wroxeter (Viroconium).

Owain Ddantgwyn 490 –520 AD
This King of Powys is claimed to have based his capital at the abandoned Roman City of Viroconium. Owain was known by his battle name 'Arth' and his father was known as 'Uthr Pen Dragon'.

Cuneglass from 520AD
The son of Owain Ddantgwyn abandoned Viroconium and probably resettled on The Wrekin.

Cynnddylan 600-658AD
This fabled Prince of Powys along with Brochmael possibly sited their Palace where Old St Chad's now stands, or at the Berth at Baschurch. 9th century Welsh poetry states that the Kings of Powys were the heirs of Great Arthur.

King Penda 626 – 655AD & King Oswald 634 – 642AD
In 642AD King Penda of Mercia defeated and killed King Oswald of Northumbria in The Battle of Maserfelth at nearby Oswestry.

King Oswy 642 – 670 AD
The brother of King Oswald defeated the Powys King Cynddylan in 658 AD at Old Oswestry Hill Fort and then plundered the kingdom.

King Offa 757 – 796 AD
The first saxon King of all the English pushed the Prince of Powys back into Wales from Shrewsbury.

In early 1929, the Sultan of Muscat stayed to be swiftly followed by the Sultan of Zanzibar in June. The following year their Imperial Highnesses the Prince and Princess Takematsu of Japan were given a tour of the town. In 1934, Abdulla Bin Ussein, the Emir of Trans-Jordan stayed and was given a tour of the town. Four years later the Ethiopian Emperor Haile Selassie visited… quite something for an English town.

shrewsbury is...

antiquated

In Shrewsbury you will find a reputable auction house, two multi-stalled antique centres and over 20 individual shops selling all manner of antiques and collectables

There's also lots you can't take home...

an early 18th century lead copy of the Farnese Hercules in Naples

shrewsbury is...

moving

Some of Shrewsbury's best features won't stay still.

☞ The statue of Hercules has had four previous settings including some time spent in a plumber's scrap yard on Wyle Cop.

☞ Near to St Julian's Friars stands a mighty obelisk to commemorate William Clement, a local dignitary. This once stood on the railway station forecourt and then moved to The Dingle.

☞ The huge and fragile Jesse Window of 1327-1353 is amongst some of the best stained glass in the country. It was originally installed at the Franciscan Friary from where it was moved to Old St Chad's. In 1792 it was moved again to its present site in St Mary's Church.

☞ The 1982 Mardol Dragon was originally painted a wonderful green. During the 1990's it disappeared to a private garage and eventually returned a dreadful shade of brown.

☞ The stone Shoemakers Arbour of 1679 can be found in The Dingle. It was originally sited where Shrewsbury School now stands.

☞ At the site of Frankwell roundabout once stood The String of Horses, a timber framed building dating from 1577. During the late 1960's it was carefully taken down and re-assembled at the Avoncroft Museum, Worcestershire.

☞ Castle Gates House, the early 17th century timber framed building situated before the Castle entrance was originally built on Dogpole.

☞ In 1812 a new peal of eight bells were hung in St Alkmund's church tower. As they caused the tower to sway, they were removed and now hang in Honolulu Cathedral.

Don't stand still – they'll get you too.

Jesse Window, St Mary's Church

William Clement's Obelisk

Shoe Makers Arbor now in the Dingle

St Andrew's Cathedral, Honalulu

Castle Gates House now stands before the Castle

The Mardol Dragon

*A little exploration on foot
will reveal the town*

John Betjeman 1956

shrewsbury is...

rural

If you want clean air and soil underfoot, you can walk to the countryside –
you don't need to find a road map first.

shrewsbury is...
natural

Shrewsbury and the countryside around it is teeming with wildlife.
It's amazing what you can find if you know where to look; try...

Monkmoor Pools –
a wetland reserve which attracts a huge number of wintering ducks and geese. In summer there are swallows and sand martins. From the hide you might be lucky enough to glimpse the skulking water rail.

Rea Brook Valley –
a Local Nature Reserve which links the countryside with the heart of the town. This green corridor is home to the flash of kingfisher blue, the silent flight of the barn owl and the splash of otters on the banks of the brook.

Tom and Luke pond-dipping near Shrewsbury

beware of the leopard...

What's that in the undergrowth? Could it be one of many sightings of big cats in the area? Reports of a wolverine and a swamp cat have been recorded.

Shrewsbury is sandwiched between the Meres and Mosses National Nature Reserve (NNR) in the north and the South Shropshire Hills Area of Outstanding Natural Beauty (AONB)

shrewsbury is...

fishing

"Pinky" a 46½ lb Shropshire Leather Carp caught by Pete Richards of Kingfisher Angling Centre, Frankwell

Some of the country's biggest carp can be found here with 40lb and even 50lb leviathans gracing the depths. Perhaps because of its inland status, enormous eels can be tempted from the tiniest of pools.

The River Severn sees salmon of up to 20lbs swimming through Shrewsbury. 20lb carp, 10lb barbel and 20lb pike have all been caught in the town. Futher upstream, shy grayling and wild trout can be found. If they prove a tad difficult to catch, plenty of trout fisheries are dotted around the county.

Shrewsbury can supply you with all your tackle and bait needs with at least three fishing shops to peruse.

Shropshire is Britain's greatest, best kept fishing secret

20lb salmon from the weir

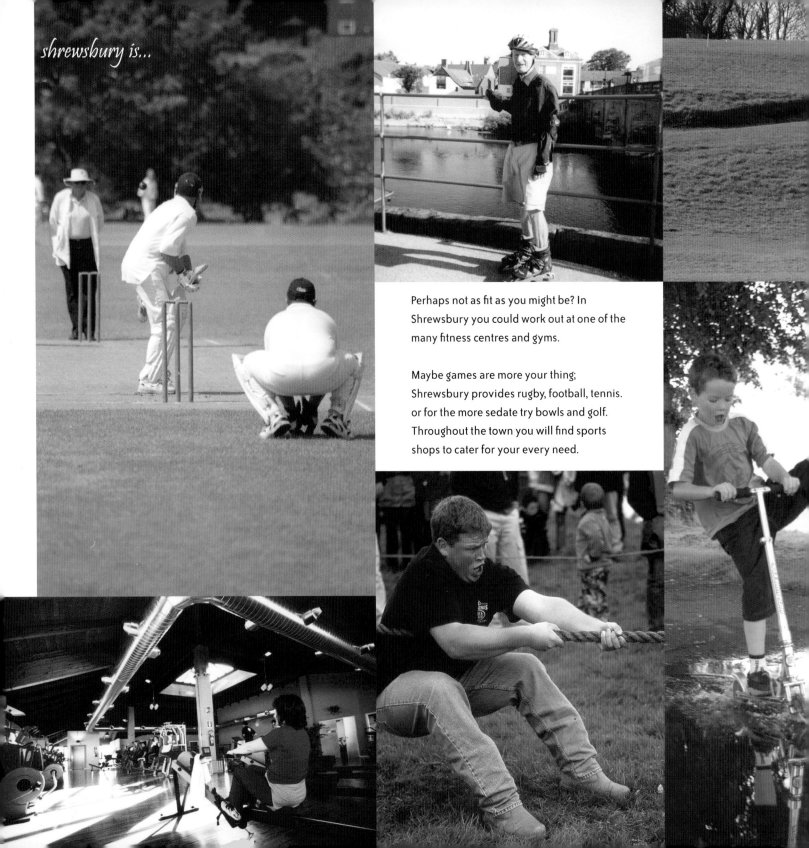

shrewsbury is...

Perhaps not as fit as you might be? In Shrewsbury you could work out at one of the many fitness centres and gyms.

Maybe games are more your thing; Shrewsbury provides rugby, football, tennis. or for the more sedate try bowls and golf. Throughout the town you will find sports shops to cater for your every need.

Sporty

shrewsbury is...
playtime

*Shrewsbury Bingo
for over thirty years*

The children's playground in Quarry Park

Balloons in the park

Kick-about
in The Quarry

Bowling at AMF,
Harlescott

Shove Ha'penny at
the Loggerheads

shrewsbury is...

safe

The feeling of safety is paramount in all of our lives.

If you feel safe you feel content

It's official: town is one of the country's safest places

SHREWSBURY has been named one of the safest towns in the country after being among the first to secure a prestigious Home Office accredited award.

The county town is the 21st town nationwide to be awarded the Business Crime Check Safe Shopping Award thanks to a range of community initiatives to crack down on crime and disorder in the main shopping areas.

The award was applied for at the beginning of last year by the Shrewsbury Retail Security Group, which then worked in partnership with town businesses, Shrewsbury Town Centre Partnership, Shrewsbury police, the borough council and other organisations to make the town a safer place to shop.

Mr Richard Goodchild, for the Shrewsbury Retail Security Group, said the town was faced with a range of criteria to be met to secure the award but two visits by representatives of the Home Office proved the hard work of town officials had paid off.

Privileged

He added:"It has been thanks to the collaboration of a range of people who have set up anything to do with crime and disorder within the town centre which would make Shrewsbury a safer place for visitors and also people employed within the town."

"We were the 21st town in the country to be privileged enough to receive the award, which is a difficult thing to achieve as you have to meet all these standards.

"We couldn't have done it without the help of Town Centre manager Fay Easton and Shrewsbury police."

Chief Superintendent Peter Wright said he was pleased the town had been recognised for all the hard work that people had put into making it a safer place.

"Everyone has worked really hard and the general public seem to be of the opinion that Shrewsbury town centre is growing in confidence.

"Our ethic was to go out there and make it a nicer place to work, shop and visit and give businesses an atmosphere in which they can flourish.

"We are not saying it is perfect but there's been an impressive transition in the past two years and there's no reason Shrewsbury shouldn't be up there with the best."

The award will be handed over to representatives of the town at 11am on Friday at the Darwin Centre when Mike Schuck, of the Home Office, makes the presentation.

CCTV in Shrewsbury Town Centre is provided in partnership between Shrewsbury & Atcham Borough Council and Severnside Housing. It is proving highly effective and is helping to make Shrewsbury a safer and more enjoyable place to visit, both during the daytime and after dark.

Local Policing Unit, West Mercia Police

Shropshire's Divisional Police Commander, Chief Superintendent Peter Wright said *"Crime and disorder is well below the national average, our initiative in partnership with the Borough Council, businesses and Town Centre Management to tackle anti-social behaviour have greatly enhanced community safety and helped the town achieve the Home Office award for 'Safer Shopping'."*

The Safer Shrewsbury Scheme

Retail businesses, pubs, clubs, police, residents and local authorities work together to make Shrewsbury crime-free.

PUB & SHOP WATCH
safer shrewsbury

shrewsbury is...

Honest

The moment that glossy pages are conceived, honesty goes out of the window; every town becomes perfect.

Finally removing the overbearing lump that was Telecom House

You never see regiments of wheely bins, pot holes disappear and public toilets are clean and abundant. Nowhere is like this.

Shrewsbury has its dodgy bits – misplaced 1960's concrete, a confusing one-way system (it's a circular town) and of course, it's famous floods. However, a forward looking local authority coupled with a strong local lobbying factor ensures that the town faces it's issues and gets results.

Not perfect, but human. People are always more important than buildings

For some, the floods were quite exciting. Duckboards through Frankwell gave a novelty to everyday life. To those directly affected it was an annual disaster (below). At long last the work on flood defences has begun (left)

odds & sods

The River Severn forms a loop around the old town – a complete ring of water for all but 275 metres of rock topped by The Castle.

30 different designs of hairpin have been found at Roman Viroconium, Wroxeter.

The annual Shrewsbury Flower Show is the World's longest-running horticultural show held continously in one location.

The commission to design the Roman Catholic Cathedral on Town Walls was won by A.W.N. Pugin, who assisted in the design of The Houses of Parliament. Unfortunately he died before starting the design.

The Buttermarket can claim to be the best World Music club in the country.

In 1628 a Shrewsbury criminal was pressed to death at the Castle.

The 1984 film 'A Christmas Carol' starring George C Scott was filmed at various locations throughout the town. One scene even showed St Paul's Cathedral at the end of Fish Street.

St Chad's Church, built in 1792, has the largest circular nave in England. It was here that Charles Darwin was christened in 1809.

Drapers Hall houses the oldest documented furniture in the country and has been associated with a continuous 500 year history in the same ownership.

Medieval Shrewsbury had an open sewer called "The Gulph" which ran from the town to "The Mudholes" near the Welsh Bridge. The effluent was used as fertiliser on nearby fields.

Properties on the old Welsh Bridge had privvies that emptied straight in to the river below, the only water supply for most people in Shrewsbury.

The population of Shrewsbury & Atcham Borough is **97,400**; its population density being twice the county average. 68% of the population live in Shrewsbury itself, although 92% of the borough is rural.

Town Population: 66,232 (2003); 23,395 (1900); 21,297(1831); Approx. 5,000 (1600); Approx. 2,500 (1550)
People in employment: 44,000 (54% women).
Shrewsbury Borough covers 230 square miles.
Shrewsbury town centre cover $\frac{1}{4}$ square mile.
90% of the population live in 10% of the space.

In 1100, Shrewsbury was the 4th largest town in England.

Shrewsbury has more shops than Bluewater with one million square feet of retail space.

During 2002 the Borough Council set wheels in motion to twin Shrewsbury with the Galapagos Islands.

Other Shrewsburys Nearby:

Shrewsbury, Massachusetts
Population (1990): 24146
Location: 42.28340 N, 71.71584 W

Shrewsbury, Missouri
Population (1990): 6416
Location: 38.58705 N, 90.32792 W

Shrewsbury, New Jersey
Population (1990): 3096
Location: 40.32660 N, 74.05973 W

Shrewsbury, Vermont
Population (1990): 1107
Location: 43.53635 N, 72.85409 W

Shrewsbury, Pennsylvania
Population (1990): 2672
Location: 39.77095 N, 76.68030 W

In the 14th century a plumber set fire to the roof of Old St Chad's, ran away and drowned in the River Severn. Divine retribution?

In 1788 the county surveyor Thomas Telford warned that the tower of Old St Chad's would soon collapse and should be taken down. His advice was ignored and the tower fell. Thomas Telford, engineering genius, yet smug.

A Victorian local celebrity, Dicky Ganderton was considered adept at the art of flogging. His system was universally approved and the constant cry of the delinquent was " oh dear Dicky!", "oh Dicky!", "not so hard Dicky!". This flogging was a common sight at the whipping post near to where the statue of Clive now stands in The Square. The last public flogging was around 1840.

Bratton's, on Dogpole, is the town's oldest music shop, founded in 1860. In 1947, Shrewsbury's John W. Bratton wrote the tune to Teddy Bear's Picnic.

In 1908 the great British composer Vaughan Williams wrote 'On Wenlock Edge'.

Shrewsbury is the only place that uses the sunken Quatrefoil as a feature of ornamentation in its timber framed buildings. It is concluded that this was the signature of an un-named craftsman working between 1570 and 1595. Examples can be seen on Owen's Mansion and Drapers Hall.

The Dingle was set out as a pleasure garden in 1719 and is now an area of peace and calm. However, it was there that on the 23rd December 1647 a local woman was found guilty of poisoning her husband and was burnt to death.

Although an English town, Shrewsbury did not become part of England until 1536. It had special status as part of the border territory of the Welsh Marches and was under control of Barons and Lords.

In 925AD Shrewsbury established a Royal Mint, producing coins for 14 English Kings, Charles I also established a Mint here.

After her US Presidential affair, Monica Lewinsky stayed at the Prince Rupert Hotel. On leaving the building and looking right, the first thing she would have seen, at the end of Butcher Row, was Clinton's, the card shop.

Shrewsbury boasts two listed letter boxes. In front of the Abbey is a Penfold Hexagonal type from the 1860's. Next to the Old Market Hall in the Square is a late 1800's octagonal type.

The narrow medieval streets were originally paved with cobble stones known as *'petrified kidneys'*.

As a visitor you can't help but notice the polite and amiable nature of the local people. In fact, it came as no surprise that in recent years, Shrewsbury was voted the friendliest town in the country.

Shrewsbury School has a 'branch' in Bangkok, Thailand.

Shrewsbury Town Football Club's most famous player was Arthur Rowley. Arthur died in 2003 and held the goal scoring record for the Football League at 434 goals in 619 games. **The record still stands**.

Two of the reasons Shrewsbury is a town and not a city are that it has no C of E Cathedral or university, although you can study for a degee. After the Reformation, the Abbey was lined up to have cathedral status with a Bishop of Shrewsbury in place... somehow it never happened.

The 1951 Castle Footbridge is Britain's first *pre-stressed, post tensioned, reinforced concrete, counter balanced cantilever bridge.*

Philip Freeman
"Shrewsbury is to quality of life what single malt is to whiskey. The lingering taste makes all the difference to the satisfaction"

Helen Peake
"It feels a safe place to bring my kids"

Peter Nutting –
Councillor
"Why would anyone want to live anywhere else?"

Terry Follette
"Having lived in Shrewsbury for over seventy years the thing I like most is that it's just the right size, not too big, not too small"

Karl Roffey
"Great buildings!"

Caroline –
Fitness First
"It's a very nice place for the summer, it's pretty, great pubs and restaurants... "

opinionated

Mel Sayers
"I like Shrewsbury because, from my home I can work, shop, sunbathe in my garden, then enjoy nightlife without ever getting in a car"

Simon McCloy –
Chief Executive,
Shropshire Tourism
"...I don't think there is anywhere else that is such an ideal place to raise a family and can offer the same quality of life"

Sarah Evans –
Shoe-b-do,
The Parade
"It's got everything, the best of both worlds – great town, great countryside"

Carl Jaycock –
Artist
"Shrewsbury for me is fascinating for its rich history and its central location in the UK, making it ideal to get to the north, south, east and west"

Cheryl Davis –
Shrewsbury
Librarian
"The Library is an amazing building to be working in"

Brian Pitts – *Elfin*
Shoes, The Parade
"I've been making hand-made shoes in Shrewsbury for 20 years, I wish I could take a holiday here"

Janet & Dave
"It's a place where you can relax"

Graham Galliers –
Property Developer
"...there's no better place to be"

Alison Patrick –
Shrewsbury Tourism Officer
"The most beautiful river and the best live music"

Richard Hewat-Jaboor – *Architect*
"I am very fortunate to live in Shrewsbury. The quality of life is amazing, it's very easy to become complacent"

Ian Cornall –
Fishmonger (centre)
"I love Shrewsbury Market because you get a lot of good people wanting real service, which I'm proud to provide"

Trevor & Chris–
Fishmongers
"We like Shrewsbury because there's plenty of totty"

Robin Hooper –
Chief Executive SABC
"...Shrewsbury is ambition"

Barbara Gillian
"There's alot going on, so much more than first meets the eye"

Paul Marsden MP
"2000 years of British history, here in Shrewsbury, waiting for you"

Alan Pryce –
Photo Focus
"It's a good size to take everything in... shopping, sightseeing and time to eat & drink... even on a Sunday"

Stephanie-Kate
"Plenty of space"

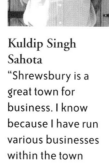

Kuldip Singh Sahota
"Shrewsbury is a great town for business. I know because I have run various businesses within the town centre for the last 16 years"

Phil Vaughan
"I've been away, but always come back. It's home"

Maggie Fisher
"I adore Shrewsbury, there are so many things to do. I would never move"

Phil Northwood & Mac
"Shrewsbury... is a way of life"

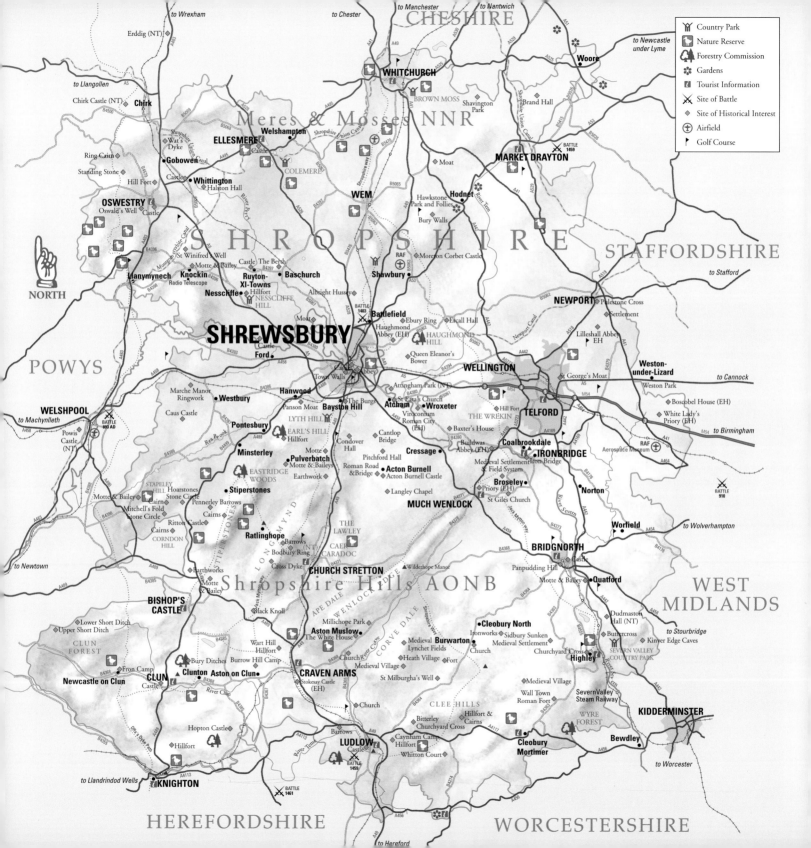

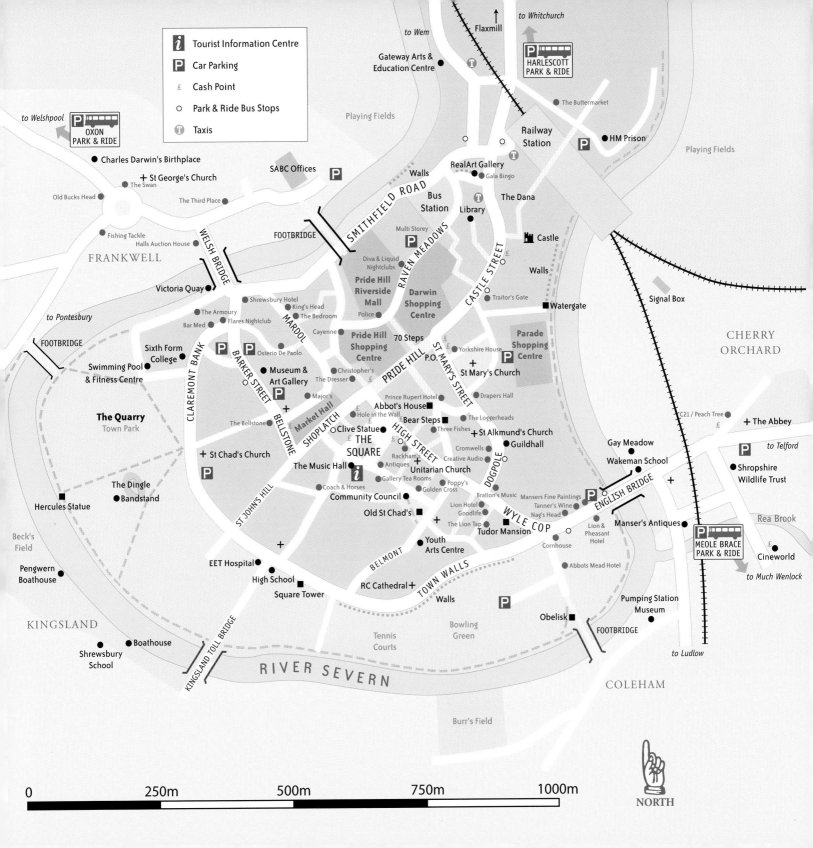

Tourist Information Centre *i*
Car Parking P
Cash Point £
Park & Ride Bus Stops O
Taxis T

to Welshpool
OXON PARK & RIDE

FRANKWELL

to Pontesbury

FOOTBRIDGE

KINGSLAND

Beck's Field

Pengwern Boathouse

Shrewsbury School

Boathouse

Hercules Statue

The Dingle
Bandstand

The Quarry
Town Park

Swimming Pool & Fitness Centre

Sixth Form College

Charles Darwin's Birthplace
St George's Church
The Swan
Old Bucks Head
The Third Place

Fishing Tackle
Halls Auction House

WELSH BRIDGE

Victoria Quay

CLAREMONT BANK

BARKER STREET

Museum & Art Gallery

The Armoury
Bar Med
Shrewsbury Hotel
King's Head
The Bedroom
Flares Nightclub
Cayenne
Osterio De Paolo

Major's

MARDOL

BELLSTONE

The Bellstone

St Chad's Church

The Music Hall
i

Coach & Horses

Community Council

ST JOHN'S HILL

EET Hospital

High School
Square Tower

KINGSLAND TOLL BRIDGE

SABC Offices
Walls
SMITHFIELD ROAD

FOOTBRIDGE

RRAVEN MEADOWS

Multi Storey
Diva & Liquid Nightclubs
Pride Hill Riverside Mall
Police

Darwin Shopping Centre

Pride Hill Shopping Centre
70 Steps

Christopher's
The Dresser

SHOPLATCH
Market Hall

Clive Statue
THE SQUARE
Rackham's Antiques
Gallery Tea Rooms

Poppy's

HIGH STREET

Hole in the Wall
Abbot's House
Bear Steps
Three Fishes

Cromwells
Creative Audio
Unitarian Church

Golden Cross

Old St Chad's

Youth Arts Centre

BELMONT

RC Cathedral

TOWN WALLS
Walls

Tennis Courts

Bowling Green

Burr's Field

RIVER SEVERN

to Wem
Flaxmill
to Whitchurch

Gateway Arts & Education Centre
T

HARLESCOTT PARK & RIDE
P

Playing Fields

The Buttermarket

Railway Station
P
HM Prison

Playing Fields

RealArt Gallery
Gala Bingo
T
The Dana
Library

Castle
Walls

CASTLE STREET
Traitor's Gate
Watergate

Signal Box

CHERRY ORCHARD

Yorkshire House
P.O.
ST MARY'S STREET
St Mary's Church
Drapers Hall

Parade Shopping Centre
P

C21 / Peach Tree
The Abbey

Prince Rupert Hotel
The Loggerheads
St Alkmund's Church
Guildhall

DOGPOLE

Gay Meadow
Wakeman School

Shropshire Wildlife Trust

to Telford

Bratton's Music
Mansers Fine Paintings
Tanner's Wine
Nag's Head
Lion Hotel
Goodlife
The Lion Tap

WYLE COP

ENGLISH BRIDGE

Manser's Antiques

Lion & Pheasant Hotel
Cornhouse

Tudor Mansion

Abbots Mead Hotel

MEOLE BRACE PARK & RIDE
P

Rea Brook

Cineworld

to Much Wenlock

Obelisk

FOOTBRIDGE

Pumping Station Museum

to Ludlow

COLEHAM

NORTH

0   250m   500m   750m   1000m

information

This book attempts to give an overall impression of a truly beautiful and fascinating place. Please find out more by visiting, seeing or reading…

Global links to Shrewsbury

The People's Network
Search the internet, email your friends and family, word process your letters, CVs etc, computers for children… All free at Shrewsbury Library, Reference and Information Service, Castle Gates, Shrewsbury.
Phone or call to book a session, ask about guided sessions for beginners.
Tel: 01743 255380/255300

Tourist Information Centre
The Square, Shrewsbury SY1 1LH
Tel: 01743 281200 Fax: 01743 662883
Email: tic@shrewsburytourism.co.uk
www.shrewsburytourism.co.uk
www.shropshiretourism.info
www.virtual-shopshire.co.uk
www.visitheartofengland.com

Entertainment
www.31days.co.uk
Cinema
www.cineworld.co.uk
Cineworld, Old Potts Way, Shrewsbury
Tel: 01743 240350
Theatre & Live Music
www.musichall.co.uk
www.shrewsburytheatre.co.uk
www.stagecoach.co.uk
Jazz & Roots Club: www.jazzandroots.com
Other Entertainments
www.amfbowling.co.uk

Attractions
www.english-heritage.org.uk
www.nationaltrust.org.uk
www.shrewsburyflowershow.org.uk
www.ironbridge.org.uk
www.hoofarm.com
www.weston-park.com
www.rafmuseum.com
www.hawkstone.co.uk
www.river-king.co.uk
www.hawkstone-hall.com
www.west-mid-show.org.uk
www.steaminsalop.co.uk
www.lolc.org.uk

Museums
Shrewsbury Museum & Art Gallery
Rowley's House, Barker Street, Shrewsbury
Tel: 01743 361196
Shrewsbury Museums Service
www.shrewsburymuseums.com
www.darwincountry.org
Shrewsbury Castle & Shropshire Regimental Museum
Castle Foregate, Shrewsbury
Tel: 01743 358516
Coleham Pumping Station
Longden Coleham, Shrewsbury
Tel: 01743 361196

Churches
St Mary the Virgin, Shrewsbury is in the care of The Churches Conservation Trust
www.visitchurches.org.uk
The Abbey, Abbey Foregate
www.shrewsburyabbey.com

Shopping
The smartest place to shop - Shrewsbury Town Centre
www.smartshrewsbury.com
Shopping Centres
www.darwincentre.co.uk
www.pridehill.co.uk
Sunday Market at Harlescott Park & Ride, 10-4pm
Shrewsbury Market Hall [Indoor Market]
Open Tuesday, Wednesday, Friday & Saturday

Food & Drink
www.smartshrewsbury.com - *the finest food guide in town - an on-line* 'Eat Out in Shrewsbury' *directory*
www.tanners-wines.co.uk
www.wroxetervineyard.co.uk
www.maynardsfarm.co.uk
www.heff.co.uk

Arts
Visual Arts Network
www.vanetwork.co.uk
Youth Arts
Belmont Arts Centre, 5 Belmont, Shrewsbury SY1 1TE.
Tel: 01743 243755
(Video and sound studios available for hire)
Andrew Logan Museum
www.andrewlogan.com

Shrewsbury Accommodation
www.prince-rupert-hotel.co.uk
www.abbotsmeadhotel.co.uk
www.sandfordhouse.co.uk
www.lionandpheasant.co.uk
www.regalhotels.co.uk/thelion
www.goldencrosshotel.co.uk
www.jdweatherspoon.co.uk
www.sydneyhousehotel.co.uk
www.restawhileinshrewsbury.co.uk
www.abbeycourt.org
www.tudorhouseshrewsbury.co.uk
www.164bedandbreakfast.co.uk
www.meolebracehall.co.uk
www.antonhouse.supanet.com
www.fieldsideguesthouse.co.uk
www.thestiperstones.com
www.abbeylodgeshrewsbury.co.uk

Library
Castle Gates, Shrewsbury Tel: 01743 255380
Email: ris.enquiries@shropshire-cc.gov.uk
www.shropshire-cc.gov.uk/library.nsf

Local Books available from
Powney's, St Alkmund's Square
Waterstones, High Street
WH Smith, Pride Hill
Tourist Information Centre, The Music Hall, The Square
www.shropshirebooks.co.uk

Local Authorities
Shrewsbury & Atcham Borough Council (SABC) Main Switchboard: 01743 281500
www.shrewsbury.gov.uk
Shropshire County Council Information Point
Tel: 01743 255303
www.shropshire-cc.gov.uk
www.shropshireonline.gov.uk

Shrewsbury and Atcham MP

3rd Floor, Talbot House, Market Street,
Shrewsbury SY1 1LF.
Tel: 01743 341422

Police

Non Emergency (24 hours) Tel: 08457 444888
Non Emergency for hearing impaired (24 hours)
Tel: 08456 000303
Shrewsbury Police Station Tel: 01743 232888
West Mercia Crime Stoppers Tel: 0800 555111
www.westmercia.police.uk

Hospital

The Royal Shrewsbury Hospital Tel: 01743 261000

Countryside & Environment

Shropshire Wildlife Trust
193 Abbey Foregate, Shrewsbury SY2 6AH
Tel: 01743 284280 Fax: 01743 284281
www.shropshirewildlifetrust.org.uk
The Greenfrog Consultancy
Email: agreenfroggy@yahoo.co.uk
Countryside Volunteer Centre Tel: 01743 350708

Community Information

www.askollie.org.uk

Transport

Shropshire County Council Public
Transport Information Tel: 0870 608 2 608
Dial a Ride Transport service Tel: 01743 450270
Shropshire Hills Shuttles
www.Shropshirehillsshuttles.co.uk
Shopmobility in Shrewsbury
Manual and powered wheelchairs and scooters available to
hire for anyone who needs help to get around Shrewsbury
Town Centre. Tel: 01743 236900
National Rail Enquiry Service Tel: 08457 484950
National Express Coaches Tel: 0870 580 8080
Arriva Buses www.arriva.co.uk

Property

www.shropshire-homes.com
www.christophermorris.net
www.coopergreen.co.uk
www.martinmonk.co.uk
www.hallsestateagents.co.uk
www.parrylowarch.co.uk
www.dbroberts.co.uk
www.samuelwood.co.uk
www.connells.co.uk
www.douglasdavies.co.uk
www.pooks.co.uk
www.barbers-online.co.uk
www.nockdeighton.co.uk
www.millerevans.co.uk

Business

Shrewsbury Town Centre Management
Partnership
SMART BUSINESS, The Victorian Wing, 20 Dogpole
Shrewsbury SY1 1ES.
Tel: 01743 246988
www.stcmp.com
www.smartshrewsbury.com
Shrewsbury Business Chamber
Tel: 01743 233000
www.shrewsburybusiness.com
Shropshire Chamber of Commerce
Tel: 01952 208200
www.shropshire-chamber.co.uk
Business Link Shropshire
Tel: 0845 754 3210
www.bl-shropshire.co.uk
Economic Development at SABC
Tel: 01743 281014
liz.dand@shrewsbury.gov.uk

Newspapers & Magazines

Smart Shrewsbury [quarterly]
Tel: 01743 246988
Axcess SHROPSHIRE Magazine [fortnightly]
www.axcessmag.com Tel: 01743 719303

Shrewsbury Chronicle [Weekly]
Tel: 01743 248248
Shropshire Star [Daily]
Tel: 01743 248248
The Shropshire Magazine
Tel: 01952 242424
Shropshire Life
Tel: 01785 220510

Radio

BBC Radio Shropshire [96 FM]
Reception Tel: 01743 248484
Shropshire's Beacon Radio [103.1 FM]

Printing & Publishing

Livesey Ltd. Printer
Tel: 01743 235651 Fax: 01743 232944
MA Creative Graphic Designers
Tel: 01743231261 www.macreative.co.uk

Details correct as of 2003

Acknowledgements

Photography

Danny Beath Photography
www.smilingleafimages.co.uk
Chris Nottingham
www.7Studios.co.uk
Mike Ashton
www.macreative.co.uk
John Hawkins
DJ Houlston
info@houlstonphotography.co.uk

Ben & Polly Osborne
www.benosbornephotography.co.uk
David Turner
Al Smith & Helen Peake
Fay Easton
Michael Pooley
Fitness First
AMF Bowling
Martin Smith
Gala Bingo
Jim Sadler
Ruth Gibson

Thanks to everyone who contributed, including:

*Mike Stokes, Shrewsbury Museums Service,
James Lanyon, Pat from STCMP, Gareth Williams,
Francesca Griffith, Bernard Martin, John Hughes,
Gary Morgan, Cheryl Davis, The Walters Family.*

shrewsbury is...

risqué

THREE HUNDRED MEN ABOARD
AND I HAVE TO GET WRECKED
WITH THIS!

Stroll down Grope Lane, visit The Bedroom in Mardol, take a look in the window of 'Naughty but Nice' ***...smile in Shrewsbury... it's a way of life***